# Fulfilling GOD'S Purpose FOR Your Life

*Judy,*
*I pray this book will encourage you in your walk with Jesus.*

## Bonnie Hammer

*Love,*
*Bonnie Hammer*

*My Life Verse*
*II Chronicles 16:9*
*NASB*

**PALADIN PUBLISHING**

Unless otherwise indicated, all Scripture quotations are taken from the *New American Standard Version* of the Bible. Scripture taken from the NEW AMERICAN STANDARD BIBLE, © 1960, 1962, 1963, 1968, 1971, 1973, 1975, 1977, 1995 by the Lockman foundation. Used by permission.

Scripture quotations marked NKJV are taken from the *New King James Version* pf the Bible. Copyright © 1982 by Thomas Nelson, Inc. Used by permission. All rights reserved.

Scripture quotations marked AMP are taken from *The Amplified Bible, New Testament,* or *The Amplified Bible, Old Testament. Copyright © 2015 by The Lockman Foundation, LaHabra, CA 90631.* All rights reserved.

*The Scripture quotation* marked TPT is taken from *The Passion Translation.* Copyright © 2017, 2018, 2020 by Passion & Fire Ministries, Inc. Used by permission. All rights reserved. ThePassionTranslation.com

Scripture quotations marked NIV are taken from *The Holy Bible, New International Version.* Copyright © 1973, 1978, 1984 by International Bible Society.

The Scripture quotation marked NCV is taken from *The Holy Bible, New Century Version.* Copyright © 1987, 1988, 1991 by Word Publishing. All rights reserved.

Scripture quotations marked MSG are taken from *The Message Bible.* Copyright © 1993, 2002, 2018 by Eugene H. Peterson. All rights reserved.

Scripture quotations marked NLT are taken from *The Holy Bible, New Living Translation.* Copyright © 1996, 2004, 2007, 2015 by Tyndale House Foundation. Used by permission of Tyndale House Publishers, Inc., Carol Stream, IL 60188. All rights reserved.

The Scripture quotation marked TLB is taken from *The Living Bible.* Copyright © 1971 by Tyndale House Foundation. Used by permission of Tyndale House Publishers, Inc., Carol Stream, IL 60188. All rights reserved.

*Fulfilling God's Purpose for Your Life*
ISBN 978-1-7360332-6-5
Copyright © 2022 by Bonnie Hammer
9908 N 120th East Ave
Owasso OK. 74055

Published by Paladin Publishing
P. O. Box 700515
Tulsa, OK 74170

Text Design: Lisa Simpson

Printed in the United States of America. All rights reserved under International Copyright Law. No part of this publication may be reproduced, stored in a retrieval system, or transmitted in any form or by any means—electronic, mechanical, photocopy, recording, or any other—except for brief quotations in printed reviews, without prior permission of the publisher.

# Dedication and Acknowledgments

I dedicate this book to the love of my life, my wonderful husband Jerry. He has been my constant encouragement and has always believed in my ability to communicate the truth of God's Word. I love you so much.

I want to thank Pastor Tom Dillingham for being obedient to give me a prophetic word a few years ago. As I was talking to him, he said he could see books and asked if I'd ever considered writing a book. This confirmed what I already knew I was to do.

One of the requirements for graduation from XploreNations Bible College was to write a fifty-page paper. Thank you, Russ and Judi Jo Adams, for the motivation to write as that paper became the basis for this book.

There are numerous others who have encouraged me in this journey, but I specifically want to mention Stephanie Solberg, a dear friend who at a ladies' retreat several years ago said I should write a devotional. The word resonated within me, and I've never forgotten it.

Thank you to Pam Woodson, another dear friend and author, who read this manuscript and gave me some advice on changes I should make as well as gave me ideas on how to get it published. She also encouraged me to go for it.

I would not be who I am if it weren't for my mom and dad, who are now in heaven, who prayed me into the kingdom of God and showed me the unconditional love of God. I know they are cheering me on.

Most of all, I thank my Lord and Savior, Jesus Christ, who made Himself real to me when I was a lost 18-year-old girl and gave me a purpose for life.

# CONTENTS

| | | |
|---|---|---|
| Chapter 1 | It's a Wonderful Life | 7 |
| Chapter 2 | Life Is Short so Make It Count | 9 |
| Chapter 3 | Yes! God Chose You! | 13 |
| Chapter 4 | God Wants Us to Know Our Purpose | 17 |
| Chapter 5 | Dream Delayed but Purpose Fulfilled | 21 |
| Chapter 6 | God Chooses All Kinds | 25 |
| Chapter 7 | Be Faithful Where God Has Called You | 29 |
| Chapter 8 | Feel Inadequate? You Are Not Alone | 35 |
| Chapter 9 | Forget the Past | 39 |
| Chapter 10 | Don't Let Fear Hold You Back | 43 |
| Chapter 11 | Don't Neglect the Gifts God Has Given You | 49 |
| Chapter 12 | Make the Most of Your Time | 53 |
| Chapter 13 | Don't Let Failure Stop You | 57 |
| Chapter 14 | Comparison Will Steal Your Joy | 61 |
| Chapter 15 | Satan Will Lie to You | 65 |
| Chapter 16 | God Redeems Our Failures | 69 |
| Chapter 17 | It's Not too Late | 75 |
| Chapter 18 | God's Plans Are Good and His Callings Irrevocable | 79 |
| Chapter 19 | First Things First | 83 |
| Chapter 20 | What Now? | 85 |
| Chapter 21 | The Lifestyle of the Chosen | 89 |
| Chapter 22 | Love and Serve Others | 95 |

| Chapter 23 | Purpose in Your Heart to Represent Jesus Well | 99 |
|---|---|---|
| Endnotes | | 105 |
| About the Author | | 111 |

# Chapter 1

# It's a Wonderful Life

One of my favorite movies, and definitely my favorite Christmas movie, is "It's a Wonderful Life." The movie is about George Bailey, a young man who had big dreams of leaving the small-town life and traveling the world. His father passes unexpectedly, and he is left to take over his father's banking business. He does so out of obligation, but he expects his brother, Harry, to come and take over the business when he comes home from college. But George is dealt another blow when Harry comes back to town with a new wife and a great job opportunity in another state. George's hopes and dreams are once again trampled. His hopes of leaving the small town of Bedford Falls are dashed again.

His uncle, Billy, who works at the bank also, through a terrible mistake, loses thousands of dollars which causes George to despair even of life. When he approaches an evil banker in town to borrow the money lost, Mr. Potter asks George what collateral he has for the loan. George offers him a life insurance policy with a cash value of $500. Mr. Potter laughs and tells George he is worth more dead than alive. George decides the only way out is to end his life so his family can collect the money.

However, in answer to the prayers of many in the town, God sends an angel named Clarence to prove to George that he really has a wonderful life. The way he does this is by showing George what the world would have been like if he had never been born. In the end, George realizes he had a great life and pleads with Clarence to let him go back to the way it was, which he did. Having been shown what a difference he had made and would make, he runs back home to his wife and children with joy and gratitude. He realized that God had a purpose for his life.[1]

Rick Warren in his best-selling book, *Purpose-Driven Life*, says, "When you understand that life is a test, you realize that nothing is insignificant in your life. Even the smallest incident has significance for your character development. Every day is an important day, and every second is a growth opportunity to deepen your character, to demonstrate love, or to depend on God. Some tests seem overwhelming, while others you don't even notice. But all of them have eternal implications."[2]

## Chapter 2

# Life Is Short So Make It Count

We may not realize what a difference we can make in this life, but it is vital that we look at our lives in the light of eternity. The Apostle Paul said, "While we do not look at the things which are seen, but at the things which are not seen. For the things which are seen are temporary, but the things which are not seen are eternal."[3]

There is a quote attributed to Mark Twain which says, "The two most important days in your life are the day you were born and the day you find out why." There is much truth in this statement. Most people have asked at some point in their life, "Why am I here?" Everyone needs to feel like they are here for a reason and that they have a purpose. I recently read that in my hometown of Tulsa, Oklahoma, the suicide rate is higher than the homicide rate. Why are so many people choosing to end their own lives? I'm sure there are many reasons, but many of them most likely could be due to lack of purpose and hopelessness. They don't see the big picture for their lives, and they don't understand that God has a special plan for them that only they can fulfill. If they did, they would see they have hope and a future.

Many years ago I read a book by Myles Munroe titled *Understanding Your Potential.* In this book he says, "The wealthiest spot on this planet is not the oil fields of Kuwait, Iraq, or Saudi Arabia. Neither is it the gold and diamond mines of South Africa, the uranium mines of the Soviet Union, or the silver mines of Africa. Though it may surprise you, the richest deposits on our planet lie just a few blocks from your house. They rest in your local cemetery or graveyard. Buried beneath the soil within the walls of those sacred grounds are dreams that never came to pass, songs that were never sung, books that were never written, paintings that never filled a canvas, ideas that were never shared, visions that never became reality, inventions that were never designed, plans that never went beyond the drawing board of the mind, and purposes that were never fulfilled. Our graveyards are filled with potential that remained potential. What a tragedy!"[4]

There is probably no place that makes us think more about eternity than a cemetery and no event that makes us think more of what the afterlife will bring than a funeral. On many headstones there is the date of birth and the date of death. Between them is a dash. That dash represents the person's life. In the light of eternity, that dash is so short. Scripture says our lives are a vapor or a mist—here today and gone tomorrow.[5] Sir Thomas Browne said, "The created world is but a small parenthesis in eternity." Everything we can see, handle, taste, and touch is temporary except mankind.

Harry Morant has said, "Live every day as if it were going to be your last; for one day you're sure to be right." David the psalmist was keenly aware of how short his life was and prayed, "Lord, remind me how brief my time on earth will be. Remind me that my days are numbered—how fleeting my life is. You have made my life no longer than the width of my hand. My entire lifetime is just a moment to you; at best, each of us is but a breath."[6]

Are we going to rob the world by not realizing our potential? Wouldn't it be better to discover God's purpose for our lives and exhaust everything God has placed within us by realizing our full potential? I want to die empty, don't you?

The parable of the talents in Matthew 25:14-30 is referring to how we are to use the money God has entrusted to us, but it can also be used to encourage us to use the gifts and abilities God has given us. The parable teaches us that God always gives us everything we need to do what He has called us to do.

## Chapter 3

# Yes! God Chose You!

Our lives change when we realize why we are on this planet. We didn't just happen, and we surely did not come from monkeys! God made a decision to give life to us. God knew us before we were ever born. Scripture says, "Before I formed you in the womb I knew you. . . ."[7] Another translation says, "Before I shaped you in the womb, I knew all about you. Before you saw the light of day, I had holy plans for you."[8] Psalm 139 is well-known for explaining God's intricate creation of us. "For You formed my inward parts; You wove me in my mother's womb. I will give thanks to You, for I am fearfully and wonderfully made; wonderful are Your works, and my soul knows it very well. My frame was not hidden from You, when I was made in secret, and skillfully wrought in the depths of the earth; Your eyes have seen my unformed substance;

and in Your book were all written the days that were ordained for me, when as yet there was not one of them."[9] Another Bible version paraphrases verse 16: "You saw me before I was born and scheduled every day of my life before I began to breathe. . . ."[10] Yet another Scripture says, "The Lord called me before my birth; from within the womb he called me by name."[11]

We didn't come from our parents. We came through our parents. Our parents may have chosen to have a child, but it is ultimately in God's hands if a child is conceived and brought to birth. Even if your parents did not plan your birth, God has a destiny for your life. No one is a mistake.

It is obvious from these verses and so many more throughout the Word of God that God knew us before we were ever born, He formed us in our mother's womb, and He has a destiny for us. Doesn't this thrill you? God designed us and planned for us to live on this earth at this crucial time in history and has a specific plan for our lives. You are not a mistake, and you are not an accident.

Not only did God know us before we were born and create us in our mother's womb, but He chose us to be His and has a plan for our life. Scripture says, "You did not choose Me but I chose you, and appointed you that you would go and bear fruit, and that your fruit would remain. . . ."[12] Another Scripture says, "For we are His workmanship, created in Christ Jesus for good works, which God prepared beforehand so that we would walk in them."[13]

The word translated "workmanship" is the Greek word *poiema* from which we get the words poem and poetry. *The New American Standard Bible* uses the word "workmanship." You could say we are God's work of art. We are His special creation.

The word "prepared" comes from the Eastern custom of sending servants in advance of a king to prepare the road ahead. Jesus said, "My sheep hear My voice, and I know them, and they follow Me."[14] Jesus leads us. In other words, He goes before us. God has already gone before us and prepared the works He wants us to do, and He has prepared the way. He knows the end from the beginning. He will get us where we need to go as we follow Him. We don't have to determine our destiny; we just need to discover it.

Scripture says, "And we know that God causes all things to work together for good to those who love God, to those who are called according to His purpose. For those whom He foreknew, He also predestined to become conformed to the image of His Son. . . ."[15] Many people quote the first half of verse 28, but the rest is so important. God will work everything for good to those who are "called according to His purpose." Every experience we have in life can be used by God in the fulfillment of our destiny.

The Apostle Paul said, "For God is working in you, giving you the desire and the power to do what pleases Him."[16] *The Amplified Bible* helps us understand the verse even better. "For it is [not your strength, but it is] God who is effectively at work in you, both to will and to work [that is, strengthening, energizing, and creating in you the longing and the ability to fulfill your purpose] for His good pleasure."[17] God actually gives us the desire to obey Him.

Scripture says, "Delight yourself in the Lord, and He will give you the desires of your heart."[18] Some people believe this verse is saying God will give us what we want, but I believe He is saying that if we are delighting ourselves in Him, He will implant His desires in our hearts. In that way He gives us the desires He wants us to have.

**Chapter 4**

# God Wants Us to Know Our Purpose

God wants us to know our purpose. The word "purpose" is defined as, "The reason for which something is created or for which something exists." One of the most popular Christian books in recent years has been *The Purpose-Driven Life* by Rick Warren. Why was it such a best seller? Because it struck a chord with so many people. We have an innate desire to know there is more to life than getting up and going to work every day, watching television, and going through the routine or life. We all want to know our lives matter. Scripture says, "For everything, absolutely everything . . . got started in him and finds its purpose in him."[19] The first step to knowing our purpose is to know our purpose-filled God!

Scripture says, "To everything there is a season, a time for every purpose under heaven."[20] For God's purposes to come to fulfillment on this earth, we must know OUR purpose because He has chosen to accomplish His will through us. "Depths of purpose and layers of meaning saturate everything you do."[21]

William James said, "The great use of life is to spend it for something that will outlast it." When you know your purpose, it gives you passion. You wake up every morning with anticipation. Mark Batterson, a well-known Christian author, said, "I have an unshakeable sense of destiny because I know that as long as I pursue God's calling on my life, then God is ultimately responsible for getting me where He wants me to go." [22]

Rick Warren says, "You were made *by* God and *for* God—and until you understand that, life will never make sense. It is only in God that we discover our origin, our identity, our meaning, our purpose, our significance, and our destiny. Every other path leads to a dead end."[23] Thomas Carlyle has said, "The man without a purpose is like a ship without a rudder – a waif, a nothing, a no man."

There are many biblical examples of men and women who fulfilled their purpose, and we continue to read their stories thousands of years later. Abraham was called on by God to leave everything and go to a land that God would show him. He later became the father of the

Hebrew nation and father of our faith. To fulfill God's purpose, he had to leave everything he had ever known and walk into the future trusting God alone.

## Chapter 5

# Dream Delayed but Purpose Fulfilled

Joseph's story, which is recorded in chapters 37-50 of the book of Genesis, is amazing. He was his father's favorite son and because of this he was hated by his brothers. He made the mistake of sharing his dream with them that they would someday bow down to him. This led to even more jealousy. When he was seventeen, they plotted to kill him by throwing him in a pit, then tell their father a wild animal had killed and devoured him. But Reuben, one of his brothers, encouraged the rest of them to put him down in a pit in the ground with the intention of coming back later to save him. In the meantime, a caravan of Ishmaelites came by on their way to Egypt. The brothers decided not to kill him, but instead, they sold him as a slave at a time Reuben was not there to save him.

Potiphar, an Egyptian officer of Pharaoh, bought him from the Ishmaelites. Joseph had great favor with God and Potiphar noticed it. He made Joseph overseer in his house and left all he owned in Joseph's charge. He was attractive and one day Potiphar's wife approached him and wanted him to lie with her, but he refused. In her anger, she lied and told Potiphar and the other men of the house that Joseph had tried to lie with her.

This made Potiphar furious, so he put him in prison. But even in prison, Joseph could not be kept down. The Lord continued to be with him and showed him grace and kindness and gave him favor with the warden. While in prison, he interpreted the dreams of a cupbearer and the baker to the king. Joseph was accurate and asked the cupbearer to remember him, but he did not.

Two years later Pharaoh had a dream that needed interpretation. No one could interpret it. Finally, the cupbearer remembered Joseph and told Pharaoh about him. He was brought before Pharaoh and accurately interpreted the dream. Because of this Joseph was set over all the land of Egypt. When the famine occurred that God had warned Pharaoh of in the dream, Joseph's family was in great need. Because of Joseph's high-ranking position, he was able to save his family as well as the Jewish people.

When his brothers came before Joseph, fearing their lives because of what they had done to him, he said, "As for you, you meant evil against me, but God meant it for good in order to bring about this present result, to preserve many people alive."[24] Joseph realized that God had a purpose in all he had gone through. He had gone from preferential treatment by his father, to the pit, to Potiphar's house, to prison, and ultimately to the palace. He recognized that all of his life had been a preparation for the position he now had and the purpose for his life to save his family and his people.

## Chapter 6

# God Chooses All Kinds

One of my favorite verses regarding purpose is about King David. Scripture says David served the purpose of God in his generation.²⁵ What better thing could be said of any of us? David was far from perfect, but he was known as "a man after God's own heart." *The Living Bible* says, "After David had served his generation according to the will of God. . . ."²⁶ Not only was he anointed to be the king of Israel and the author of most of the Psalms, but he was also chosen to be in the lineage of our Savior, Jesus Christ.

The Apostle Paul, before his conversion on the road to Damascus, was a persecutor of the Church. He was on his way to kill Christians when Jesus appeared to him. After this encounter, Jesus spoke to Ananias and told him to lay hands on Paul. Ananias was fearful because he knew how Paul was persecuting believers. But the Lord said, "Go, for he is a chosen instrument of Mine, to bear My name before the Gentiles and kings and the sons of Israel; for I will show him how much he must suffer for My name's sake."[27]

Paul was well aware of how gracious God was to save him and call him. Paul said, "I thank Christ Jesus our Lord, who has strengthened me, because He considered me faithful, putting me into service, even though I was formerly a blasphemer and a persecutor and a violent aggressor. And yet I was shown mercy because I acted ignorantly in unbelief; and the grace of our Lord was more than abundant, with the faith and love which are found in Christ Jesus. It is a trustworthy statement, deserving full acceptance, that Christ Jesus came into the world to save sinners, among whom I am foremost of all."[28]

The fact that Paul knew Jesus did not prevent him from undergoing great persecution himself, but his life's mission became to serve Jesus with his whole heart no matter what the cost. As he was anticipating his martyrdom in a Roman prison, he wrote his last letter to Timothy. In this letter he said, "I have fought the good fight, I have finished the course, I have kept the faith."[29] Paul was ready to die knowing he had fulfilled God's purpose for his life. It had not been an easy road, but he said in the next verse, "In the future there is laid up for me the crown of righteousness, which the Lord, the righteous Judge, will award to me on that day; and not only to me, but also to all who have loved His appearing."[30] All the pain, suffering, and persecution had been worth it to know he had completed what his Savior had called him to do.

If God could take a hater and persecutor of Jesus Christ and His Church, and save him and use him to bring salvation to the Gentiles and write much of the New Testament, don't you think He can use you?

Our ultimate example of someone who lived every day of His life with a divine purpose and mission is our Lord Jesus. His entire life led up to Him giving His life as a sacrifice. As He neared the end of His earthly life, He prayed, "I glorified You on the earth, having accomplished the work which You have given Me to do."[31] Jesus did everything His Father had planned for Him to do and, in so doing, brought glory to God. Then on the cross, as He was dying, He exclaimed, "It is finished."[32] The price had been paid for our salvation. His purpose was fulfilled. When we fulfill our purpose, it brings glory to God.

**Chapter 7**

# Be Faithful Where God Has Called You

What does purpose look like for you? You may be called to the fivefold ministry as an apostle, prophet, evangelist, pastor, or teacher. God may call you to serve as a missionary to an unreached people group. You may be called to work in your local church as a youth leader, a children's director, to head up a men's or women's group, to help in a food pantry, to teach a Sunday school class, or any number of other ministries.

The Apostle Paul wrote, "Take heed to the ministry which you have received in the Lord, that you may fulfill it."[33] *The New Living Translation* of this verse says, "Be sure to carry out the ministry the Lord gave you."[34] It is important to be faithful to do what He has called us to do.

Your calling may be to work in the secular world. Your mission field may be a co-worker or your boss who needs a godly influence. There may be many opportunities to be a light in the darkness. Some people work in Christian environments, but if God has you in a worldly environment, rejoice! You may be the only Jesus some of those you work with will ever see. You have a purpose there! Scripture says, "Whatever you do, do your work heartily as for the Lord rather than for men."[35] We need to remember that we are actually serving the Lord – not men.

Are you a stay-at-home mom? Scripture says, "Children are a gift of the Lord. . . ."[36] I believe being a mom and raising children is the greatest calling a woman can have. A mother is influencing not just her children, but the generations that will follow. Tony Campolo is a well-known sociologist, pastor, author, and public speaker, whom we first heard many years ago at a youth conference. He told how his wife would sometimes be asked in a condescending way what she did for a living, as if being a mother was not enough. She decided when she would be asked this question, she would respond in this way: "I am socializing two homo sapiens in the dominant values of the Judeo-Christian tradition in order that they might be instruments for the transformation of the social order into the eschatological utopia that God willed from the beginning of creation." I have a feeling they wouldn't have a response to that!

You may be in a time in your life when you are a caregiver for an elderly parent or relative. Your responsibility may be raising a special needs child. Sometimes a person in these roles can begin to feel overwhelmed and feel like they would like to be out really making a difference. Trust me – you are making an amazing difference! Not everyone is called to be out in front of people, but it can be hard when you seldom have time to get out by yourself.

I read a quote by a lady named Ruth Harms Calkin years ago that I felt was so powerful I wrote it on the inside of my Bible. "You know, Lord, how I serve You with great emotional fervor in the limelight. You know how eagerly I speak for You at a Women's Club. You know my genuine enthusiasm at a Bible study. But how would I react, I wonder, if You pointed to a basin of water and asked me to wash the calloused feet of a bent and wrinkled old woman day after day, month after month, in a room where nobody saw and nobody knew?"

The thing is – God sees. Even if no one else does. Everything we do, whether other people see it or not, should be done for God and His glory. This life is not about us; it is about Him and us doing what He is asking us to do. Some day we will stand before God and be asked, "What did you do with what I gave you?" Are we being faithful stewards of the gifts and abilities God has given us?

But what if you don't feel qualified? What if you don't think God has something special for you? Maybe you haven't had much education or came from a poor family. Maybe you feel insecure and don't feel like God could use you. What if you feel like you don't have anything to offer? Some people grow up with feelings of inadequacy and worthlessness which causes them to feel like they will never amount to anything. These are all things that can hinder you from believing God has something special for you. But Paul is clear in I Corinthians about the kind of people God is looking for. "Just look at your own calling, believers; not many [of you were considered] wise according to human standards, not many powerful or influential, not many of high and noble birth. But God has selected [for His purpose] the foolish things of the world to shame the wise [revealing their ignorance], and God has selected [for His purpose] the weak things of the world to shame the things which are strong [revealing their frailty]. God has selected [for His purpose] the insignificant (base) things of the world, and the things that are despised and treated with contempt, [even the things that are nothing, so that He might reduce to nothing the things that are, so that no one may [be able to] boast in the presence of God."[37]

## Chapter 8

# Feel Inadequate?
# You Are Not Alone

God often chooses people that the world would dismiss. When Samuel went to Jesse's house to reveal who would be anointed king of Israel, Jesse brought all his sons before him – all except David. As the sons were brought before Samuel, the Lord spoke to him and said, "God sees not as man sees, for man looks at the outward appearance, but God looks at the heart."[38] After all the sons had been brought before Samuel, he asked Jesse if those were all his children. Jesse answered that there was one left – the youngest – and he was tending the sheep. Samuel asked that he be brought to him. Samuel then anointed him in the midst of his brothers, and the Spirit of the Lord came mightily upon David from that day forward. Here was the youngest son, a shepherd, being anointed to become the king of Israel. There is no reaction recorded by David, but I'm sure he probably thought, "Me?" My guess is he probably felt somewhat inadequate and probably pondered these things in his heart for many days.

David is not the only person chosen by God who the world would not have chosen for certain things, but God sees our heart and the potential in all of us. Gideon is another example of someone who felt inadequate. While he was beating out wheat in the winepress in order to save it from the Midianites, the angel of the Lord appeared to him, and said, "The Lord is with you, O valiant warrior."[39] I'm sure Gideon looked around to see who the angel was talking to because surely he wasn't talking to him! The angel went on to say, "Go in this your strength and deliver Israel from the hand of Midian. Have I not sent you?"[40]

Gideon then goes on to give all the reasons why God must have the wrong man. "O Lord, how shall I deliver Israel? Behold, my family is the least in Manasseh, and I am the youngest in my father's house."[41] God was not going to be deterred. Gideon was His man – inadequacies and all—but God promised to be with him. Gideon followed through, and his people were delivered from the Midianites.

## Feel Inadequate? You Are Not Alone

If you feel inadequate to do anything for God, you are not alone. God sees beyond your real or perceived insecurities and inadequacies and wants to use you to do something great for Him. One of the men God used in the most powerful way ever was Moses who struggled with great insecurity. When God appeared to him in the burning bush and called him to deliver His people, Moses questioned, "Who am I, that I should go to Pharaoh, and that I should bring the sons of Israel out of Egypt?"[42] He also questioned, "What if they will not believe me or listen to what I say?"[43] But Moses really shows his insecurities in verse 10: "Please, Lord, I have never been eloquent, neither recently nor in time past, nor since You have spoken to Your servant; for I am slow of speech and slow of tongue."[44]

Moses felt very inadequate to fulfill what God was asking of him and had all kinds of excuses, but God was not going to withdraw His calling from Moses' life. Instead, God promised to be with him. "Now then go, and I, even I, will be with your mouth, and teach you what you are to say."[45] But even after this, Moses still pleaded with God to send someone else. You would think if God would appear to you in a burning bush and speak directly to you that you would immediately obey. But not Moses. He was doubting his own abilities to do what God had called him to.

However, we know that eventually Moses followed through and led his people out of Egyptian bondage, and he is listed in Hebrews 11 as a great man of faith. We can learn from this that it doesn't matter how inadequate we feel or how many excuses we may have, God will not relent on our calling.

## Chapter 9

# Forget the Past

Some people feel they cannot be used of God because of their past. In John 4 we read about the Samaritan woman with a troubled past. As Jesus was traveling to Galilee, He passed through Samaria and sat down by a well as He was weary from His journey. A woman from Samaria came to draw water, and Jesus asked her for a drink. She questioned Him why He would ask her for a drink since He was a Jew, and the Jews did not have anything to do with the Samaritans.

Jesus replied, "If you knew the gift of God, and who it is who says to you, 'Give me a drink,' you would have asked Him, and He would have given you living water."[46] Their conversation continued, and Jesus told her things about herself that there was no way He should have known. She realized He was the Christ—the Messiah—and left her waterpot and went into the city and declared, "Come, see a man who told me all the things that I have done; this is not the Christ, is it?"[47]

Many of the Samaritans believed in Him because of her testimony. Some of them went to Jesus and asked Him to stay with them which He did for two days. Many more believed because of His word that they heard for themselves. The Samaritan woman impacted many people.

God used this woman who had had five husbands and was living with another. I'm sure she felt unworthy of true love and acceptance and probably felt like this was her lot in life, until Jesus came to her. It didn't matter what she had done or what she had been through, God wanted to use her. He had a purpose for her.

Do you feel like there are things in your past that should prevent you from being all God wants you to be? The Apostle Paul said, "Brethren, I do not regard myself as having laid hold of it yet; but one thing I do: forgetting what lies behind and reaching forward to what lies ahead, I press on toward the goal of the prize of the upward call of God in Christ Jesus."[48]

To fulfill our purpose, we must be willing to let go of our past failures and press toward the goal before us. A Scripture in Isaiah says, "Do not call to mind the former things, or ponder the things of the past. Behold, I will do something new, now it will spring forth; will you not be aware of it? I will make a roadway in the wilderness, rivers in the desert."[49] Isaiah also says, "Behold, the former things have come to pass, now I declare new things; before they spring forth, I proclaim them to you."[50] God wants to do a new thing in your life. It is time to let go of the past and go after all God has for you. We are products of our past, but we don't have to be prisoners of it.

# Chapter 10

# Don't Let Fear Hold You Back

Fear is a stronghold that can hold people back from experiencing God's best for them. The Apostle Paul wrote, "God has not given us a spirit of fear, but of power and of love and of a sound mind."[51] We can experience fear of the unknown, fear of failure, or fear of what others think of us. When Paul wrote this letter to Timothy, Paul was in a Roman prison anticipating his soon coming death for his faith. This was during a great time of persecution for the Church. Timothy had every right to feel fearful or timid, but Paul reminds him that God is not the One who gives us a spirit of fear. God fills us with boldness and confidence. To fulfill our purpose, we must refuse to fear!

After God had delivered the children of Israel from Egypt's bondage, the Lord spoke to Moses saying, "Send out for yourself men so that they may spy out the land of Canaan, which I am going to give to the sons of Israel; you shall send a man from each of their fathers' tribes, every one a leader among them."[52] Moses did as the Lord had commanded and told the spies to see what the land was like, whether the people were strong or weak, whether they were many or few. He also wanted to know if the land was good or bad and if the cities were fortified. Moses asked them to find out if the land was fat or lean and whether there were trees and fruit.

When the spies returned from spying out the land, they came with a branch which had a single cluster of grapes. It was so large and heavy they had to use a pole carried by two men in order to bring the fruit. The fruit of the land was abundant.

They told Moses, "We went into the land where you sent us; and it certainly does flow with milk and honey, and this is its fruit. Nevertheless, the people who live in the land are strong, and the cities are fortified and very large; and moreover, we saw the descendants of Anak there."[53]

Caleb, who was one of the spies, quieted the people and said, "We should by all means go up and take possession of it, for we shall surely overcome it."[54] He was full of faith and believed God would give them the land because He had promised He would give it to them. But ten of the spies disagreed and said, "We are not able to go up against the people, for they are too strong for us."[55]

One of the other spies who believed God was Joshua. He and Caleb were filled with faith and trusted God. Others were fearful and gave a negative report because they didn't believe they could do it. They were looking at things with their physical eyes rather than with the eyes of faith. They even said they were like grasshoppers in their sight. You could say they had a "grasshopper mentality"!

Their fear and feeling of inadequacy were keeping them from stepping into God's plan and purpose for them. Instead of trusting what God had said, they allowed their emotions to defeat them. When they brought the negative report, the rest of the people cried out, wept, and grumbled against Moses and Aaron. They said it would have been better for them to die in Egypt than to become plunder for their enemies.

Joshua then spoke up and said, "If the Lord is pleased with us, then He will bring us into this land and give it to us – a land which flows with milk and honey. Only do not rebel against the Lord; and do not fear the people of the land; for they will be our prey."[56] But even Joshua, filled with faith and confidence in God, could not convince the people who now were ready to stone him and

Caleb. But the glory of the Lord appeared in the tent of meeting to all the children of Israel which prevented this.

God became so angry He was ready to smite the people with pestilence and dispossess them and make Moses a nation mightier and greater than they were. He was angry that they were choosing fear and inadequacy over faith in what He had said. But Moses interceded and saved them from being cast away, though there was a price to pay.

Since the people had chosen to believe the negative report of ten spies rather than believe the report of Caleb and Joshua, and because they cried out that they wished they had died in the wilderness, that is exactly what God gave them. Instead of entering the promised land of Canaan, all the men twenty years old and upward died in the wilderness, never seeing the promised land because of their doubt and unbelief.

God had a destiny for them, but they missed out because they did not choose to believe God and the report of Caleb and Joshua. We must trust what God's Word says about us. Don't give in to a "grasshopper mentality."

It is true that we are not adequate—or sufficient—in ourselves, but our adequacy is from God.[57] In the midst of weaknesses, insults, distresses, and persecutions, Paul realized he was not able in himself to do what God had called him to. He said, "For when I am weak, then I am strong."[58] Scripture also says, "Let the weak say, 'I am strong!'"[59] How was Paul strong? Scripture tells us. Jesus had said to him, "My grace is sufficient for you, for power is perfected in weakness. . . ."[60]

If we are trying to fulfill our purpose in our own strength we will fail. We simply cannot do it, and God never expected us to. That is why He gave us the Holy Spirit. Scripture says, "'Not by might nor by power, but by My Spirit,' says the Lord of hosts."[61]

One of the most often quoted verses says, "I can do all things through Christ who strengthens me."[62] *The Amplified Bible* translates this verse, "I can do all things [which He has called me to do] through Him who strengthens and empowers me [to fulfill His purpose – I am self-sufficient in Christ's sufficiency; I am ready for anything and equal to anything through Him who infuses me with inner strength and confident peace.]"[63]

## Chapter II

# Don't Neglect the Gifts God Has Given You

Something else that can hold us back from fulfilling our purpose is neglecting the gifts God has given us. Paul warned Timothy, "Do not neglect the spiritual gift within you. . . ."[64] The Bible is clear that God has given all of us spiritual gifts. Scripture says, "Now there are varieties of gifts, but the same Spirit. And there are varieties of ministries, and the same Lord. There are varieties of effects, but the same God who works all things in all persons. But to each one is given the manifestation of the Spirit for the common good. For to one is given the word of wisdom through the Spirit, and to another the word of knowledge according to the same Spirit; to another faith by the same Spirit, and to another gifts of healing by the one Spirit, and to another the effecting of miracles, and to another prophecy, and to another the distinguishing of spirits, to another various kinds of tongues, and to another the interpretation of tongues. But one and the same Spirit works all these things, distributing to each one individually just as He wills."[65]

The Holy Spirit gives the gifts as He chooses. Scripture says, "But now God has placed the members, each one of them, in the body, just as He desired."[66]

Paul explains the fivefold ministry gifts in Scripture: "And He gave some as apostles, and some as prophets, and some as evangelists, and some as pastors and teachers, for the equipping of the saints for the work of service, to the building up of the body of Christ; until we all attain to the unity of the faith, and of the knowledge of the Son of God, to a mature man, to the measure of the stature which belongs to the fullness of Christ."[67]

God wants to use you in the spiritual gifts listed in I Corinthians 12, and some of you may be called to the fivefold ministry, but there is another list of gifts or ministries in the book of Romans: "For just as we have many members in one body and all the members do not have the same function, so we, who are many, are one body in Christ, and individually members one of another. Since we have gifts that differ according to the grace given to us, each of us is to exercise them accordingly: if prophecy, according to the proportion of his faith; if service, in his serving; or he who teaches, in his teaching; or he who exhorts, in his exhortation; he who gives, with liberality; he who leads, with diligence; he who shows mercy, with cheerfulness."[68]

As you can see, there is a huge variety of gifts and ministries God may call you to. You will most likely operate in many of these. You may operate in a word of wisdom one day, and the next day you may be teaching or encouraging someone. All of these are important, and God wants to use us in these gifts and ministries. We must be careful not to neglect the gifts God has placed in us. He gave them to us to help others and to fulfill His purposes.

## Chapter 12

# Make the Most of Your Time

Bad time management can hinder us from fulfilling God's purpose. One way God has made us equal is in giving us all 24 hours in a day. No one has more or less time than another. The issue is in how we spend it. Scripture says, "Therefore be careful how you walk, not as unwise men but as wise, making the most of your time, because the days are evil."[69] *The Amplified Version* says, "Therefore see that you walk carefully [living life with honor, purpose, and courage; shunning those who tolerate and enable evil], not as the unwise, but as wise [sensible, intelligent, discerning people], making the very most of your time [on earth, recognizing and taking advantage of each opportunity and using it with wisdom and diligence], because the days are [filled with] evil."[70]

Do you see people around you who seem to accomplish so much? If you were to question them about how they are successful, most of them, if not all of them, have learned to manage their time well. How much time do we spend in front of the television or on the Internet? What about Facebook? I venture to say many people spend more time on social media than they do actually communicating with others. Steven Furtick says, "Most believers aren't in imminent danger of ruining their lives. They're facing a danger that's far greater: wasting them."[71]

Stephen Covey has said, "The key is not to prioritize what's on your schedule, but to schedule your priorities." Do we allow our schedule to dictate how we spend our day, or do we determine our priorities and schedule our days and lives around them? What do we put first?

We read in the Psalms, "Teach us to number our days, that we may gain a heart of wisdom."[72] We need to be consciously aware that our days are numbered, and if we want to make a real difference, we must be wise in how we spend them. Time is like money in that once it is spent, it cannot be used again. Carl Sandburg said, "Time is the most valuable coin in your life. You and you alone will determine how that coin will be spent. Be careful that you do not let other people spend it." In Ecclesiastes we read, "God has made everything beautiful for its own time. He has planted eternity in the human heart. . . ."[73] God Himself has placed within each of us a sense of eternity, but are we managing our time well in light of this?

There is a little book called *Tyranny of the Urgent,* written by Charles Hummel. The question we need to ask ourselves regularly is, "Am I investing my time in the urgent things or the important things?" There will always be demands on our time, but if we are not careful, we will spend our lives dealing with urgent things that are shouting the loudest and neglecting the important things. We must learn to be a master of our minutes.

## Chapter 13

# Don't Let Failure Stop You

Fear of failure is another thing that hinders many from reaching their full potential. Maybe you tried something and failed. Failing does not make you a failure. It is only when you never get up that you are a failure. If you have failed, it shows you stepped out and took a risk, and that is a very good thing. If you never fail, you are probably not doing much. J. K. Rowling has said, "It is impossible to live without failing at something, unless you live so cautiously that you might as well not have lived at all, in which case you have failed by default."

A young child learns to walk by taking a step, then falling, taking a step and falling, over and over. Do the parents criticize that child because they didn't walk all over the place the first time? Of course not! They are just happy the child is attempting what they have not done before. It is all a part of growing up. When the child falls, does he just sit there and cry and give up and decide to never try to walk again? No. They get back up and try again over and over until they master the skill.

When we begin to step out into God's plans for our lives, there will be risks. There will be times we make mistakes and fail, but we must have the determination to get back up and try again. Do not be discouraged that you didn't succeed; be encouraged that you were willing to take a chance on doing something new. Our greatest regrets may not be that we tried something and failed, but that we never tried at all.

We may have to leave comfort behind and take a risk with the unknown. When God called Abraham, He told him to leave everything he knew and go to a land He would show him. Change can be very uncomfortable. Steven Furtick says, "It's drastic to cut ties with the thing that is chaining you to a life you've become comfortable with. But I promise you, the real risk isn't in launching into a new life of greater things. It's staying in your old life of the ordinary."[74]

Peter is a perfect example of someone who failed. Not only did he fail, but he failed Jesus. He had told Jesus that he would die for Him, but when confronted by some who questioned him as Jesus' trial approached, he said he didn't even know Jesus. Not just once, but three times. After he denied Jesus, he went out and wept bitterly. Can you imagine how he must have felt? He had spent three years with Jesus, day and night. He had seen the mighty miracles Jesus did and had experienced His unconditional love. How could he have denied Him?

But this was not the end of Peter's story. In fact, Jesus had even told Peter, "Simon, Simon, behold, Satan has demanded permission to sift you like wheat; but I have prayed for you that your faith may not fail; and you, when once you have turned again, strengthen your brothers."[75] This is exactly what happened on the Day of Pentecost.

When the Holy Spirit fell upon the disciples in the upper room, who was it that stepped up and preached to those who had gathered in Jerusalem for Pentecost? Peter! Scripture says, "So then, those who had received his word were baptized; and that day there were added about three thousand souls."[76] Not only did he preach this great sermon, but he went on to write two letters, 1 Peter and 2 Peter, that have encouraged, challenged, and admonished believers for over two thousand years.

Despite his failure at the time Jesus needed him the most, he went on to be used mightily by God to touch multitudes of people, and we are talking about him today. Failure is not final unless we refuse to get up and try again.

## Chapter 14

# Comparison Will Steal Your Joy

A big hindrance to fulfilling God's purpose for our lives can be comparing ourselves with others. Instead of appreciating and being thankful for who God made us to be, we can compare ourselves with others. When we do, we are negating the fact that God made us the way we are and gifted us specifically for the calling He has placed on our lives.

Lisa Bevere, in her book, *Without Rival,* tells the following experience she had with the Lord. "As I was dozing off, I heard the Holy Spirit whisper, 'I do not love My children equally.' Shocked, I sat straight up in bed. Where did this blasphemous thought come from? I blurted out, 'You have to love us the same or else it wouldn't be fair.' My protest was answered with, 'I don't. Equal implies My love can be measured, and I assure you . . . it cannot. Same would mean My children are replaceable or interchangeable, and they are not. My heart is not divided into compartments. No one could take the place of or displace another in My heart. For you see, I don't love My children equally, I love them uniquely.' Take a deep breath and listen. God loves us uniquely rather than equally. Believe me, unique is better."[77]

God loves us uniquely and has a unique plan for our lives, so why would we want to be like someone else? If we are comparing ourselves with others, is it a subtle way we are telling God we don't think He did the right thing when He created us the way we are? We must realize God made us special and loves us just the way we are and wants to use us.

The Apostle Paul said, "For we are not bold to class or compare ourselves with some of those who commend themselves; but when they measure themselves by themselves and compare themselves with themselves, they are without understanding."[78] Comparison inevitably leads to envy and jealousy if we wish we were like someone else.

Here is a word God gave Jeremiah about the house of Israel, but we can apply it to our lives as well: "The word which came to Jeremiah from the Lord saying, 'Arise and go down to the potter's house, and there I will announce My words to you.' Then I went down to the potter's house, and there he was, making something on the wheel. But the vessel that he was making of clay was spoiled in the hand of the potter; so he remade it into another vessel, as it pleased the potter to make. Then the word of the Lord came to me saying, 'Can I not, O house of Israel, deal with you as this potter does?' declares the Lord. 'Behold, like the clay in the potter's hand, so are you in My hand, O house of Israel.'"[79]

God knows exactly what He is doing with each of us. There is a worship chorus that says, "Mold me and make me after Thy will, while I am waiting, yielded and still." That is a wonderful way to look at our life in God's hands. We need to allow Him to mold us and make us into what He wants so He can use us to our fullest potential.

Theodore Roosevelt said, "Comparison is the thief of joy." This is so true. We must take joy in who God made us to be instead of questioning God about why we aren't like someone else. After Jesus had died and been raised from the dead, He appeared to His disciples several times. One occasion is recorded in John 21. Jesus questions Simon Peter about whether he loves Him. Then Jesus says to him, "Truly, truly, I say to you, when you were younger, you used to gird yourself and walk wherever you wished; but when you grow old, you will stretch out your hands and someone else will gird you, and bring you where you do not wish to go."[80]

Jesus said this to explain what kind of death Peter would endure, then asked Peter to follow Him. Peter turned around and saw John and said, "Lord, and what about this man?"[81] Instead of simply following Jesus, he questioned what was going to happen to John. He was apparently not feeling like Jesus was being fair.

Jesus said, "If I want him to remain until I come, what is that you? You follow Me!"[82] I believe He is saying the same things to us. It doesn't matter what anyone else is doing or how God is using or is dealing with anyone else. Our eyes need to be on Jesus. We are to follow Him!

Comparison leads to envy and jealousy. Instead of being thankful for what God has done in our lives and desiring to find out God's plan for our lives, we are focused on how God is using others. Scripture says, "For where jealousy and selfish ambition exist, there is disorder and every evil thing."[83] One version says there is confusion and every evil work. When we compare ourselves to others, it will cause strife, jealousy, and confusion. Aren't these enough reasons to let go of comparison?

## Chapter 15

# Satan Will Lie to You

Our enemy, Satan, wants to hinder or stop us from fulfilling our purpose. In Scripture he is called "the devil and Satan, who deceives the whole world. . . ."[84] Jesus says of the devil, "He was a murderer from the beginning, and does not stand in the truth, because there is no truth in him. Whenever he speaks a lie, he speaks from his own nature, for he is a liar and the father of lies."[85]

Satan will lie to us in many ways. One of those ways is in accusations. Revelation 12:10 calls him the "accuser of the brethren." The battlefield really is the mind. He will throw accusations against us. He will bring up our past sins, failures, and mistakes to try to get us to shrink back. But we must stand firm in our faith and on the Word of God. Scripture says, "Therefore there is now no condemnation for those who are in Christ Jesus."[86] It doesn't matter what we have done in the past; it is covered by the blood and we are forgiven. We stand before God righteous because of what Jesus did for us.

The devil will try to convince us that we are not worthy to be used. It is true that in and of ourselves, we are not worthy. But we have been ransomed and redeemed, and God paid a great price for us by sending His Son, Jesus.

The Apostle Paul makes it clear that we are not called because of our status in life or because there is something great in ourselves. "For consider your calling, brethren, that there were not many wise according to the flesh, not many mighty, not many noble; but God has chosen the foolish things of the world to shame the wise, and God has chosen the weak things of the world to shame the things which are strong, and the base things of the world and the despised God has chosen, the things that are not so that He might nullify the things that are, so that no man may boast before God."[87] Steven Furtick says, "God doesn't do greater things exclusively through great people. He does them through anyone who is willing to trust Him in greater ways."

In the Word, Paul makes it plain that he was not chosen because he deserved it. "I thank Christ Jesus our Lord, who has strengthened me, because He considered me faithful, putting me into service; even though I was formerly a blasphemer and a persecutor and a violent aggressor. Yet I was shown mercy because I acted ignorantly in unbelief; and the grace of our Lord was more than abundant, with the faith and love which are found in Christ Jesus. It is a trustworthy statement, deserving full acceptance, that Christ Jesus came into the world to save sinners, among whom I am foremost of all."[88]

Paul did not try to defend himself against Satan's accusations by telling Satan what great things he had done. He knew he had been forgiven and that there was no condemnation for him since he was in Christ. No matter what our past, we can stand against the onslaught of the enemy in boldness and confidence realizing it is not about us, but about our Savior who paid the price for us.

When we step out to do what God has called us to do, the enemy is not going to sit back and let it happen without a fight. He knows what fate awaits him, but in the meantime, he will try to wreak as much havoc as possible and try to hinder us. Many doors to preach the Gospel had opened for Paul, but he said, "A wide door for effective service has opened to me, and there are many adversaries."[89]

It wasn't an easy road for Paul. He details some of the challenges he faced as he obeyed God's directions: "Are they servants of Christ? – I speak as if insane – I more so; in far more labors, in far more imprisonments, beaten times without number, often in danger of death. Five times I received from the Jews thirty-nine lashes. Three times I was beaten with rods, once I was stoned, three times I was shipwrecked, a night and day I have spent in the deep. I have been on frequent journeys, in dangers from rivers, dangers from robbers, dangers from my countrymen, dangers from the Gentiles; dangers in the city, dangers in the wilderness, dangers on the sea, dangers among false brethren; I have been in labor and hardship, through many sleepless nights, in hunger and thirst, often without food, in cold and exposure. Apart from such external things, there is the daily pressure on me of concern for all the churches."[90]

Despite Paul being called to bring the Gospel to the Gentiles, he had to endure much persecution and natural circumstances. But he kept going. He didn't quit. He wrote in his letter to the Philippians, "I press on toward the goal for the prize of the upward call in Christ Jesus."[91] He didn't allow anything to stop him, and neither should we. We must keep on keeping on to complete everything God has for us regardless of the attacks the enemy sends against us.

## Chapter 16

# God Redeems Our Failures

Failure and a concern it's too late keep some people from doing what they are called to do. It is never too late to do what God has said. It doesn't matter what your age is, how you may have failed or gotten off track, God still wants to use you.

Peter had denied Jesus and watched Him die on the cross. He knew he had failed Jesus. How could he have turned away from this close friend and the one he believed was the Son of God? Despite his failures, Jesus was ready to use him in ways Peter couldn't have ever thought possible.

After Jesus' resurrection and His appearance to many afterwards, He manifested Himself to the disciples while they were at the Sea of Tiberias. Peter said to the other disciples, "I am going fishing."[92] The rest of them joined him, and despite fishing all night, they caught nothing. When morning came, Jesus stood on the beach and said, "Children, you do not have any fish, do you? . . . Cast your net on the right-hand side of the boat and you will find a catch."[93] They did as He said and gathered so many fish they couldn't haul them all in.

Up until this point, they did not realize it was Jesus who had spoken to them. But John said to Peter, "It is the Lord."[94] Peter, being the impulsive one, jumped into the sea and swam to shore. The other disciples came in the boat dragging the net full of fish.

When they reached land, they realized Jesus had prepared a charcoal fire and the fish were already placed on it; and there was also bread, so Jesus and disciples ate together. When they had finished, Jesus asked Peter, "Do you love Me more than these?"[95] There are varying opinions of what "these" are. I personally believe He is talking about fish and fishing as an occupation. Then Jesus spoke to him and said, "Tend my lambs."[96]

Jesus was showing him that no matter what he had done, He still wanted to use him. He still had a purpose for his life. This story has such a rich and deep meaning, but it is good to dig a little deeper to see the higher significance.

Luke 5 tells the story of when Jesus got into one of Peter's boats and asked him to take the boat away from the land because there were so many people. He needed a place to preach from. He sat down and began to teach, and when He was finished, He said, "Put out into the deep water and let down your nets for a catch."[97]

Peter questioned Him, but did as He said, and when he did, so many fish were brought into the net that he had to call others to help, and they filled both of the boats so they started to sink. When Peter saw this, he fell down at Jesus' feet and said, "Go away from me, Lord, for I am a sinful man, O Lord!"[98]

This is the first recorded instance where Peter called Jesus "Lord." He had seen the power of God on display and when he did, it caused him to have an awareness of his sinfulness which made him fall at His feet.

If we look forward to the events in John 21, what were the disciples doing? They were fishing and catching nothing. It is almost a repeat of what had happened in Luke 5. I believe God was reminding Peter of the first time he really understood who Jesus was.

But what other correlations are there to John 21 and Peter's life? Despite the fact the disciples obeyed His word and caught a multitude of fish, what was Jesus doing when they got to shore? He was cooking fish on a charcoal fire. If we look back at Peter's recent days, where was he when he denied Jesus?

John 18 tells of Judas' betrayal of Jesus and Jesus being brought before the priests. Scripture says, "Simon Peter was following Jesus, and so was another disciple. Now that the disciple was known to the high priest and entered with Jesus into the court of the high priest, but Peter was standing at the door outside. So the other disciple, who was known to the high priest, went out and spoke to the doorkeeper, and brought Peter in. Then the slave who kept the door said to Peter, 'You are not also one of this man's disciples, are you?' He said, 'I am not.' Now the slaves and the officers were standing there, having made a charcoal fire, for it was cold and they were warming themselves; and Peter also was with them, standing and warming himself."[99]

Peter has denied Jesus once up to this point. Where was he? Standing and warming himself by a charcoal fire. Scripture says, "Now Simon Peter was standing and warming himself. So they said to him, 'You are not also one of His disciples, are you?' He denied it, and said, 'I am not.' One of the slaves of the high priest, being a relative of the one whose ear Peter cut off, said, 'Did I not see you in the garden with Him?' Peter then denied it again, and immediately a rooster crowed."[100]

Three times Peter denied Jesus, and all three times he was near a charcoal fire. Now Jesus has cooked fish and invited Peter to eat around a charcoal fire. I believe Jesus was reaching out to Peter letting him know that He was very aware of Peter's denial, but He had forgiven him and wanted to use him now to reach multitudes.

Think about this. Peter had denied Jesus three times. How many times did Jesus ask Peter if he loved Him? Three times. Where had Peter been when he first called Jesus "Lord" and understood who He was? When they had fished all night and caught nothing. Jesus told them to drop down their nets, and the nets were filled with fish. Now the same thing has happened again. It's almost like Jesus is saying, "Remember, Peter. Remember who I am. Remember when you had the revelation of who I am. I am still the same Lord you professed."

Now by the charcoal fire, I believe Jesus is revealing to Peter that despite his failures and denial that he even knew Jesus, there was forgiveness. Jesus never gave up on Peter. It didn't matter what he had done, Jesus still had a plan for him.

## Chapter 17

# It's Not Too Late

Sometimes people, as they get older, think it is too late to be used of God. The Bible speaks so clearly to this issue. Abraham was 100 years old and Sarah was 90 when their son, Isaac, was born through whom came the Jewish race. Moses was 80 years old when he led the people of Israel out of Egypt.

Joyce Meyer, author and speaker, was 42 years old when she began her ministry. The late Lester Sumrall, pastor and evangelist, started Lester Sumrall Evangelistic Association when he was 44 and established a humanitarian aid organization, Feed the Hungry, when he was 74.

There are many other individuals who began their most effective ministries later in life. If you are older, you may never start an actual ministry, but you can minister every day. The need is great among younger people to have someone speak into their lives. Older people have an opportunity to make a big difference to the next generations.

When Paul wrote to Titus, he spoke of the need for older men and women to be examples. "Older men are to be temperate, dignified, sensible, sound in faith, in love, in perseverance. Older women likewise are to be reverent in their behavior, not malicious gossips or enslaved to much wine, teaching what is good, so that they may encourage the young women to love their husbands, to love their children, to be sensible, pure, workers at home, kind, being subject to their own husbands, so that the word of God will not be dishonored."[101]

Some have the mistaken idea that once men and women have reached a certain age their usefulness to society and church is lessened. Nothing could be further from the truth. God wants us, as we age, to hopefully gain much wisdom that we can pass on to the next generation. Scripture says, "Great is the Lord, and highly to be praised; and His greatness is unsearchable. One generation shall praise Your works to another, and shall declare Your mighty acts."[102]

Paul had called young Timothy to travel with him and minister alongside him, but the time came for Paul's life to come to a close. He would soon be called to give his life for the preaching of the Gospel. Second Timothy records his last known written words to Timothy. Before he dies, he wants to make sure Timothy understands that it is now up to him to carry the truth to the next generation. Paul said, "You therefore, my son, be strong in the grace that is in Christ Jesus. The things which you have heard from me in the presence of many witnesses, entrust these to faithful men who will be able to teach others also."[103]

You may be young and in the prime of your life. There is so much you can accomplish for God. In your case, be bold to step out into what God is speaking to your heart. Paul warned Timothy, who was young at the time, "Let no one look down on your youthfulness, but rather in speech, conduct, love, faith and purity, show yourself an example of those who believe."[104]

Jeremiah was called when he was young, and he replied to God, "'Alas, Lord God! Behold, I do not know how to speak, because I am a youth. But the Lord said to me, 'Do not say, "I am a youth." Because everywhere I send you, you shall go. And all that I command you, you shall speak. Do not be afraid of them, for I am with you to deliver you,' Declares the Lord."[105]

God's Word is clear that no matter who you are, how old you are, or what your past has been, He still wants to fulfill His purpose through your life!

## Chapter 18

# God's Plans Are Good and His Callings Irrevocable

Jeremiah 29:11 is a very well-known verse. "For I know the thoughts that I think toward you, says the Lord, thoughts of peace and not of evil, to give you a future and a hope."[106] God has not lost sight of His plan for you!

Romans 11:29 says, "For the gifts and calling of God are irrevocable."[107] *The Amplified Version* says, "For the gifts and the calling of God are irrevocable [for He does not withdraw what He has given, nor does He change His mind about those to whom He gives His grace or to whom He sends His call]."[108] Once God places a gift and calling on us, it is there forever. We may walk away from it or fail along the way, but His plans do not change.

Scripture says, "So I will restore to you the years that the swarming locust has eaten, the crawling locust, the consuming locust, and the chewing locust."[109] Even though we hear it said we can't get time back, God can still restore time. He is the only One who can redeem time.

We must realize what our part is and what God's part is. We have the promise in Philippians 1:6 that God will finish what He has started in us. He is always working in us even when we can't see it. Another scripture in Philippians says, "For it is God who is at work in you, both to will and to work for His good pleasure."[110] He actually gives us the desire to do His will. We don't come up with that on our own. He is involved in every detail of our lives.

*The Amplified Version* of this verse says, "For it is [not your strength, but is is] God who is effectively at work in you, both to will and to work [that is, strengthening, energizing, and creating in you the longing and the ability to fulfill your purpose] for His good pleasure."[111]

A scripture in the Psalms says, "The Lord will accomplish what concerns me. . . ."[112] The word for "accomplish" is *gamar* in Hebrew. It means to accomplish, perfect, and perform. God will perform His plan in our lives. He will finish what concerns us.

## Chapter 19

# First Things First

But what is our part? The first step is making sure we have a relationship with Jesus. The Word of God says we have all sinned and fall short of the glory of God. That includes everyone from the late Billy Graham to the worst sinner you can think of. We have all sinned. Scripture says, "For the wages of sin is death, but the free gift of God is eternal life in Christ Jesus our Lord."[113]

There is nothing we can do in ourselves to be right with God. We cannot do enough good works which is why God sent Jesus to die for us. Another scripture says, "But God demonstrates His own love toward us, in that while we were yet sinners, Christ died for us."[114] And a scripture in John says, "For God so loved the world, that He gave His only begotten Son, that whoever believes in Him shall not perish but have everlasting life."[115]

What do we need to do in order to be saved? "But as many as received Him, to them He gave the right to become children of God, even to those who believe in His name."[116] We receive Him by confessing we believe He is who He says He is and invite Him into our life. "If you confess with your mouth Jesus as Lord, and believe in your heart that God raised Him from the dead, you shall be saved; for with the heart a person believes, resulting in righteousness, and with the mouth he confesses, resulting in salvation."[117]

God is ready and willing to receive anyone who comes to Him. Scripture says, "For whoever will call upon the name of the Lord will be saved."[118] It's not about our works; it's about His grace for scripture says, "For by grace you have been saved through faith; and that not of yourselves, it is the gift of God; not as a result of works, so that no one may boast."[119]

## Chapter 20

# What Now?

Once we have settled our relationship with God, we can take the next steps. These are not in a specific order, but there are some things we need to do to accomplish His plan for us. Scripture says, "Commit your works to the Lord, and your plans will be established."[120] *The Amplified Bible* says, "Commit your works to the Lord [submit and trust them to Him], and your plans will succeed [if you respond to His will and guidance]."[121] We must commit ourselves to Him and His plan. The Word also says, "The mind of man plans his way, but the Lord directs his steps."[122] How can we ensure that our plans and God's plans are lining up?

It is vital that we seek the Lord in prayer and through His Word. Spending time in fellowship with Him and communion will bring clarity to our vision. Once we know what He wants for us, it is important to write it down. Scripture directs us to "Write the vision and make it plain on tablets, that he may run who reads it. For the vision is yet for an appointed time; but at the end it will speak, and it will not lie. Though it tarries, wait for it; because it will surely come, It will not tarry."[123]

Another thing we must do in order to fulfill God's purpose for our life is to be connected to others. Every believer is a part of the body of Christ. We each have our own place and gifting, our own weaknesses and strengths, and we don't have a right to say we don't need other believers. Scripture says, "But our bodies have many parts, and God has put each part just where he wants it. How strange a body would be if it had only one part! Yes, there are many parts, but only one body. The eye can never say to the hand, 'I don't need you.' The head can't say to the feet, 'I don't need you.'"[124]

We need each other to complete what God is asking of us. It is so true that no man is an island, and that is never truer than in the body of Christ. The Word says, "As iron sharpens iron, so one person sharpens another."[125] The Bible has many verses that talk about "one another." We are to pray for one another, encourage one another, build each other up, admonish one another, teach one another, spur one another to good deeds, serve one another, be kind to one another, and be devoted to one another in brotherly love.

It has been said that if you see a turtle on top of a fence post, you know he didn't get there on his own. He had help. It is the same way in our lives. Sometimes we are the ones who need someone to help us, but other times we are the ones to help someone else. There are people connected to your call, just as there are people on the other side of your obedience.

It is important that we attend church services regularly, but most of the time there is not much time to really get to know one another. This is why small groups are so important. When the Holy Spirit was poured out on the Day of Pentecost, thousands of people were saved. How did these new believers grow in their walk with Jesus? "They were continually devoting themselves to the apostles' teaching and to fellowship, to the breaking of bread and to prayer. Everyone kept feeling a sense of awe; and many wonders and signs were taking place through the apostles. And all those who had believed were together and had all things in common; and they began selling their property and possessions and were sharing them with all, as anyone might have need. Day to day continuing with one mind in the temple, and breaking bread from house to house, they were taking their meals together with gladness and sincerity of heart, praising God and having favor with all the people. And the Lord was adding to their number day by day those who were being saved."[126]

These new believers were living with a sense of community. They studied the Word together, they prayed together, they ate meals together, and they met from house to house. They needed each other – as do we.

## Chapter 21

# The Lifestyle of the Chosen

As I have talked about fulfilling God's purpose for our lives, I have focused on our individual callings and giftings. But in the life of a believer, there are some plans God has for every one of His children. They could be considered more of a general call.

Besides receiving Jesus as our Savior as I shared earlier, we must also surrender our lives to God. The Word says, "So you also should consider yourselves to be dead to the power of sin and alive to God through Christ Jesus."[127] We are to offer our lives to Him – wholeheartedly and without reservation. The Word also says, "Therefore I urge you, brethren, by the mercies of God, to present your bodies a living and holy sacrifice, which is your spiritual service of worship. And do not be conformed to this world, but be transformed by the renewing of your mind, so that you may prove what the will of God is, that which is good and acceptable and perfect."[128]

At the end of Paul's life, as he was reflecting on his service and surrender to God, he was able to say to his spiritual son, Timothy, "For I am already being poured out as a drink offering, and the time of my departure has come. I have fought the good fight, I have finished the course, I have kept the faith; in the future there is laid up for me the crown of righteousness, which the Lord, the righteous Judge, will award to me on that day; and not only to me, but also to all who have loved His appearing."[129] Paul had lived a surrendered life. It had not been an easy road, but it had been a fulfilling one.

Christlikeness is also a goal we should all strive for. Scripture says God predestined us to become conformed to the image of His Son.[130] God's purpose for us is that we be His representatives on this earth. Jesus was perfect love, grace, and mercy. We should be following His example and allowing these characteristics to flow from our lives.

One of the greatest ways we reflect Jesus to this world is by loving each other and loving people of the world. Scripture says, "Beloved, let us love one another, for love is from God; and everyone who loves is born of God and knows God. The one who does not love does not know God, for God is love."[131]

In scripture Paul lists the qualities of a believer who has allowed the Holy Spirit to develop His fruit in his life. "But the fruit of the Spirit is love, joy, peace, patience, kindness, goodness, faithfulness, gentleness, self-control; against such things there is no law."[132]

Jesus is no longer walking on this earth, but God has poured out His Spirit into our lives so we can walk the same way Jesus did, not only in our character, but in miracle-working power. In fact, Jesus said ,"Truly, truly, I say to you, he who believes in Me, the works that I do, he will do also; and greater works than these he will do; because I go to the Father."[133] When Jesus walked this earth, He trained His disciples to "heal the sick, raise the dead, cleanse the lepers, cast our demons. . . ."[134] He expected them to do the same things He did. That was part of their calling. They were to be fishers of men telling them about salvation, but they were to also demonstrate the power of God to the world. He expects us to do the same.

When Paul wrote to the Corinthian church, he told them he didn't come with fancy words, but with the demonstration of the Gospel. "My message and my preaching were not in persuasive words of wisdom, but in demonstration of the Spirit and of power, so that your faith would not rest on the wisdom of men, but on the power of God."[135]

After Jesus had died and had been resurrected, He said to His disciples before He ascended to the Father, "All authority has been given to Me in heaven and on earth. Go therefore and make disciples of all the nations, baptizing them in the name of the Father and the Son and the Holy Spirit."[136] Another time, after the resurrection, Jesus appeared to the disciples and said, "Go into all the world and preach the gospel to all creation."[137] The verses in Matthew are known to many as "The Great Commission." It is not "The Great Suggestion."

This was the way that God's ultimate plan and purpose would be fulfilled – by taking the Gospel to the ends of the earth. Jesus prophesied about the outpouring of the Holy Spirit that was to come by saying, "But you will receive power when the Holy Spirit has come upon you; and you shall be My witnesses both in Jerusalem, and in all Judea and Samaria, and even to the remotest part of the earth."[138]

If our goals, plans, and dreams do not further the Gospel of Jesus Christ, we have gotten off course. Jesus said He had come to seek and save the lost. Ultimately He came to save lost humanity, but He also came to save other things that had been lost. Jesus said, "As the Father has sent me, I am sending you."[139] He has done His part; now it is our turn.

When Adam and Eve fell into sin in the Garden, they lost their close and intimate relationship with their Father. When Jesus died and was raised, He made a way for us to come back to Him and have intimate fellowship with Him. In a sense, God had lost His man, Adam, but Jesus had come to get His man back!

## Chapter 22

# Love and Serve Others

A crucial part of our calling is to not only love people but to love God. When Jesus was asked, "What is the greatest commandment?" He replied by saying, "Love the Lord your God with all your heart and with all your soul and with all your strength."[140] This is our number one command. If we miss this, we have missed it completely. Everything we do should flow out of our love and passion for Jesus. Keith Wheeler, evangelist, said in a class I took many years ago, "Ministry is simply the overflow of a life lived in love with Jesus." If we love Jesus, we will love as He did.

Another area in the general purpose of God is serving others. Jesus said, "The Son of Man did not come to be served, but to serve, and to give His life a ransom for many."[141] Even though He was God, He laid His deity and privileges aside and became a servant. We are to have the same attitude. "Have this attitude in yourselves which was also in Christ Jesus, who, although He existed in the form of God, did not regard equality with God a thing to be grasped, but emptied Himself, taking the form of a bond-servant, and being made in the likeness of men. Being found in appearance as a man, He humbled Himself by becoming obedient to the point of death, even death on a cross."[142]

Paul refers to himself many times as a bondservant of Jesus Christ. In Exodus, God is speaking to Aaron and Miriam because they had murmured against Moses, and He says, "Not so, with My servant Moses, he is faithful in all My household; with him I speak mouth to mouth, even openly, and not in dark sayings, and he beholds the form of the Lord. Why then were you not afraid to speak against My servant, against Moses?"[143] What greater compliment could we have than to be called a servant of the Lord?

We are called to serve one another in love. We can have all kinds of ideas and plans about what we want to do for God, but if we are not serving others, we are missing it. Scripture says, "For you were called to freedom, brethren; only do not turn your freedom into an opportunity for the flesh, but through love serve one another."[144] When we use our spiritual gifts, we are serving others. "As each one has received a special gift, employ it in serving one another as good stewards of the manifold grace of God."[145]

A Danish proverb says, "What you are is God's gift to you; what you do with yourself is your gift to God." As we give ourselves to serve God and others, we will be fulfilling God's general purpose for our lives. We will be called to do specific things, but if service is not involved, we are not really fulfilling God's perfect plan.

Speaking to the elders of the church at Ephesus, Paul said, "The most important thing is that I complete my mission, the work that the Lord Jesus gave me."[146] *The Message Bible* says, "What matters most to me is to finish what God started: the job the Master Jesus gave me of letting everyone I meet know all about this incredibly extravagant generosity of God."[147]

# Chapter 23

# Purpose in Your Heart to Represent Jesus Well

We are now Christ's representatives. Scripture says, "Therefore, we are ambassadors for Christ, as though God were making an appeal through us; we beg you on behalf of Christ, be reconciled to God."[148] An ambassador is someone who goes to a foreign country and represents the king or leader. This is not really our home. Our citizenship is in heaven.[149]

In the Word we read, "But you are a chosen race, a royal priesthood, a holy nation, a people for God's own possession, so that you may proclaim the excellencies of Him who has called you out of darkness into His marvelous light."[150] He chose us to be His own possession to proclaim who He is and His goodness.

While He was on the earth, Jesus said He was the light of the world, but He also said, "You are the light of the world. A city set on a hill cannot be hidden."[151] We live in a dark world, but we are the lights leading the way to Jesus. Another scripture says, "So that you will prove yourselves to be blameless and innocent, children of God above reproach in the midst of a crooked and perverse generation, among whom you appear as lights in the world, holding fast the word of life. . . ."[152]

If we want to fulfill God's destiny for our lives, we must be people of the Word of God and prayer. God's Word says, "For the word of God is living and active and sharper than any two-edged sword, and piercing as far as the division of soul and spirit, of both joints and marrow, and able to judge the thoughts and intentions of the heart."[153] The Word of God helps us determine if our thoughts are coming from our own mind and emotions or from the Spirit of God.

The more Word we have stored up in our hearts, the easier it is for God to reveal His plan to us. Scripture says, "Your word is a lamp to my feet and a light to my path."[154] God has revealed much of His will and direction in His Word. If we sense God calling us to do something and it doesn't line up with scripture, it is not Him. He will never contradict His Word.

Prayer is crucial also if we want to make sure we are hearing God correctly. As we commune with Him and have fellowship with Him through prayer, He will speak to our heart and to our spirit. He will confirm things by giving us His peace. Scripture says, "Let the peace of Christ rule in your hearts, to which indeed you were called in one body; and be thankful."[155] This word "rule" is the same word that would be used for an umpire in a ball game. Let God's peace be the umpire in your life as you make decisions.

To be used by God in a mighty way, we must be willing to start where we are. Jesus said, "He who is faithful in a very little thing is faithful also in much. . . ."[156] Why should God give further light to someone who is not walking in the light he already has? If we are not faithful in the small things, God will not entrust larger things to us. When we get to the end of our lives, what is it we want Jesus to say to us? "Well done, my good and faithful servant."

Ephesians contains a very familiar verse to most Christians: "Now to Him who is able to do far more abundantly beyond all that we ask or think, according to the power that works within us."[157] Some people stop with the first part of the verse, but the last part is vital to understanding what Paul is saying here. God is able to do more than we could ever imagine through US because of the power that is within us.

We will accomplish God's plans and purposes as we seek Him, pray, spend time in His Word, spend time in a community of believers, use the gifts we have been given, and spend our time wisely. If we have confessed our sins to God, we need to let go of any shame or guilt that tries to hold us down. We must let go of our past mistakes and failures, and allow God to show us how He still wants to use us. We must push past any fear, feelings of inadequacy, or inferiority and realize God has a unique plan for us. Comparison has no place in our lives if we want to accomplish everything He has called us to.

There is nothing more fulfilling than knowing we are making a difference in this life. Just as George Bailey in the movie, "It's a Wonderful Life," came to a point in his life that he thought there was no real value to his life, sometimes we doubt God could do anything with our lives.

But I am here to tell you that God still has a wonderful life for you – filled with purpose, satisfaction, joy, peace, and direction. I pray that you will allow Him to do a deep work in your heart so you can see how very loved and valuable you are to Him, His kingdom, and those around you.

I would ask you to do this. Put your hand over your heart and hear your heartbeat. It is saying, "Purpose! Purpose! Purpose!" God has a wonderful plan and purpose for your life regardless of how old you are or what you have been through. You have gifts and abilities God wants to use to touch the lives of many people. You are here on purpose, and you have a purpose. May we all live purpose-filled lives.

# Endnotes

Chapter 1
[1] *It's a Wonderful Life,* Liberty Films, 1946.
[2] Warren, Rick. *The Purpose-Driven Life,* Grand Rapids, MI: Zondervan, 2002.

Chapter 2:
[3] 2 Corinthians 4:18 NKJV
[4] Munroe, Myles. *Understanding Your Potential,* Destiny Publishers, 1991.
[5] James 4:14
[6] Psalm 39:4-5 NLT

Chapter 3:
[7] Jeremiah 1:5
[8] Jeremiah 1:5 MSG
[9] Psalm 139:13-16
[10] Psalm 139:16 TLB
[11] Isaiah 49:1 NLT
[12] John 15:16
[13] Ephesians 2:10
[14] John 10:27
[15] Romans 8:28-29
[16] Philippians 2:13 NLT
[17] Philippians 2:13 AMP
[18] Psalm 37:4

Chapter 4:
[19] Colossians 1:16 MSG
[20] Ecclesiastes 3:1 NKJV
[21] Psalm 92:5 TPT
[22] Batterson, Mark. *In a Pit with a Lion on a Snowy Day,* Multnomah Books, 2006.
[23] Warren, Rick. Op. Cit.

Chapter 5:
[24] Genesis 50:20

Chapter 6:
[25] Acts 13:36
[26] Acts 13:36 TLB
[27] Acts 9:15-16
[28] 1 Timothy 1:12-15
[29] 2 Timothy 4:7
[30] 2 Timothy 4:8
[31] John 17:4
[32] John 19:30

Chapter 7:
[33] Colossians 4:17
[34] Colossians 4:17 NLT
[35] Colossians 3:23
[36] Psalm 127:3
[37] 1 Corinthians 1:26-28

Chapter 8:
[38] 1 Samuel 16:7
[39] Judges 6:12
[40] Judges 6:14
[41] Judges 6:15
[42] Exodus 3:11
[43] Exodus 4:1
[44] Exodus 4:10
[45] Exodus 4:12

Chapter 9:
[46] John 4:10
[47] John 4:29
[48] Philippians 3:13-14
[49] Isaiah 43:18-19
[50] Isaiah 42:9

Chapter 10:
[51] 2 Timothy 1:7 NKJV
[52] Numbers 13:2
[53] Numbers 13:27-28
[54] Numbers 13:30

# Endnotes

[55] Numbers 13:31
[56] Numbers 14:8-9
[57] See 2 Corinthians 3:5
[58] 2 Corinthians 12:10
[59] Joel 3:10 NKJV
[60] 2 Corinthians 12:9
[61] Zechariah 4:6
[62] Philippians 4:13 NKJV
[63] Philippians 4:13 AMP

Chapter 11:
[64] 1 Timothy 4:14
[65] 1 Corinthians 12:4-11
[66] 1 Corinthians 12:18
[67] Ephesians 4:11-13
[68] Romans 12:4-8

Chapter 12:
[69] Ephesians 5:15-16
[70] Ephesians 5:15-16 AMP
[71] Furtick, Steven. *Greater,* Colorado Springs, CO: Multnomah Books, 2012.
[72] Psalm 90:12 NKJV
[73] Ecclesiastes 3:11 NLT

Chapter 13:
[74] Furtick, Steven. Op. Cit.
[75] Luke 22:31-32
[76] Acts 2:41

Chapter 14:
[77] Bevere, Lisa. *Without Rival,* Grand Rapids, MI: Revell, 2016.
[78] 2 Corinthians 10:12
[79] Jeremiah 18:1-6
[80] John 21:18
[81] John 21:21
[82] John 21:22
[83] James 3:16

Chapter 15:
[84] Revelation 12:9

[85] John 8:44
[86] Romans 8:1
[87] 1 Corinthians 1:26-29
[88] 1 Timothy 1:12-15
[89] 1 Corinthians 16:9
[90] 2 Corinthians 12:23-28
[91] Philippians 3:14

Chapter 16:
[92] John 21:3
[93] John 21:5-6
[94] John 21:7
[95] John 21:15
[96] John 21:15
[97] Luke 5:4
[98] Luke 5:8
[99] John 18:15-18
[100] John 18:25-27

Chapter 17:
[101] Titus 2:2-5
[102] Psalm 145:3-4
[103] 2 Timothy 2:1-2
[104] 1 Timothy 4:12
[105] Jeremiah 1:6-8

Chapter 18:
[106] Jeremiah 29:11 NKJV
[107] Romans 11:29
[108] Romans 11:29 AMP
[109] Joel 2:25 NKJV
[110] Philippians 2:13
[111] Philippians 2:13 AMP
[112] Psalm 138:8

Chapter 19:
[113] Romans 6:23
[114] Romans 5:8
[115] John 3:16

# Endnotes

[116] John 1:12
[117] Romans 10:9-10
[118] Romans 10:13
[119] Ephesians 2:8-9

Chapter 20:
[120] Proverbs 16:3
[121] Proverbs 16:3 AMP
[122] Proverbs 16:9
[123] Habakkuk 2:2-3
[124] 1 Corinthians 12:18-21 NLT
[125] Proverbs 27:17 NIV
[126] Acts 2:42-47

Chapter 21:
[127] Romans 6:13 NLT
[128] Romans 12:1-2
[129] 2 Timothy 4:6-8
[130] See Romans 8:29
[131] 1 John 4:7-8
[132] Galatians 5:22-23
[133] John 14:12
[134] Matthew 10:8
[135] 1 Corinthians 2:4-5
[136] Matthew 28:18-19
[137] Mark 16:15
[138] Acts 1:8
[139] John 20:21 NIV

Chapter 22:
[140] See Matthew 22:37
[141] Matthew 20:28
[142] Philippians 2:5-8
[143] Numbers 12:7-8
[144] Galatians 5:13
[145] 1 Peter 4:10
[146] Acts 20:24 NCV
[147] Acts 20:24 MSG

Chapter 23:
[148] 2 Corinthians 5:20
[149] See Philippians 3:20
[150] 1 Peter 2:9
[151] Matthew 5:14
[152] Philippians 2:15-16
[153] Hebrews 4:12
[154] Psalm 119:105
[155] Colossians 3:15
[156] Luke 16:10
[157] Ephesians 3:20

# About the Author

**Bonnie Hammer** has been a Bible teacher and small group leader for many years. She has taught in-depth Bible courses, spoken at ladies' retreats, and regularly posts uplifting thoughts and messages on her personal social media page. She also has a public Facebook page, Bonnie's Reflections, where she shares teachings from the Word of God.

Bonnie has been married to her husband, Jerry, since 1974. They have two sons, two daughters-in-law, and two beautiful granddaughters. She is actively involved in her church and has a passion to teach the Word of God because it is what revolutionized her life many years ago. She knows the power of God's Word and is called to teach and share the truth.

Bonnie graduated from Victory Bible Institute in Tulsa, Oklahoma, in 1994 and then later graduated from XploreNations Bible College in Broken Arrow, Oklahoma, in 2017. She believes you can never fill your mind with too much scripture as it is what transforms us and gives us the power to overcome in life.